SOMETHING IN THE TIN

Biscuits, Cakes & Breads From 30 years at Lavistown

Olivia Goodwillie
Illustrations by Kate Raggett

For my mother, Muriel,
who always has something in the tin.

Contents

	Introduction	7
BISCUITS, CAKES & SLICES	**Almond** Slices	9
	Crispy **Almond** Biscuits	11
	Spanish **Almond** Cake	13
	Honey and **Almond** Tart	15
	Banana and Walnut Squares	17
	Biscotti	19
	Easy Peasy **Brownies**	21
	Cashew Caramel Squares	23
	Cheddar Cheese Biscuits	25
	Chocolate Amaretti Cake	27
	Christmas Biscuits	29
	Citrus Cake	31
	Coconut Macaroons	33
	Coconut Slices	35
	Date Slices	37
	Lavistown **Flapjacks**	39
	Ginger Jumblies	41
	Muriel's **Gingerbread**	43
	Granola Bars	45
	Hazelnut Cookies	47
	Honey Cake	49
	Kate's **Lemon** Bars	51
	Muffins	53
	Simple **Shortbread** Biscuits	57
	Tea Brack	59
	White Chocolate and Apricot Cookies	61
BREADS	Versatile Plain Dough	65
	Lavistown Loaves	69
	Mama's Bread	71
	Versatile Rich Dough	73
	Cinnamon Swirls	75
	Hot Cross Buns	77
	Almond Ring	79

Introduction

We have been cooking for courses here at Lavistown for over thirty years and have shared many recipes with people during that time. I have also listened to many requests to put them together into a book. So here it is!

Grading
All the recipes are simple to make but I have graded them with stars: ★ is very simple, ★★ a little bit more work and ★★★ quite fiddly but worth it.

Equipment
My two main pieces of equipment are the food processor and the electric beater .
Sometimes neither is used and then you will see for a saucepan or for a bowl.

I use a 30x20x4cm straight-sided tin for all the squares and slices and a baking tray of 23x32cm with a shallow edge for making biscuits and flapjacks. Don't worry if your tins are not exactly these sizes; a smaller tin will give thicker squares and a larger one, thinner.

I use baking parchment (not greaseproof) all the time. It means you can remove even the stickiest things from the tin. If the item comes away cleanly you can use the sheet again. For shortbread bases, flapjacks, granola bars etc you can press the mixture firmly into the tin using an extra sheet of parchment under your hand.

Measurements
You will see that the measurements are given in metric as it is much easier to use than imperial. Almost all kitchen scales can be set to metric - so embrace it!

All the temperatures are given for a fan oven. If you have a non-fan oven increase the values by 10 degrees.

Ingredients
You should use caster sugar, plain all-purpose flour, large eggs and regular salted butter unless it says otherwise.

When you are making these recipes for the first time, try to be as accurate as possible. Small changes in quantities can lead to very strange results in cakes and biscuits. However, unless you burn them to a cinder, most things can be salvaged. Almost anything can be rescued by ice cream!

Enjoy the book and happy baking.

Almond Slices

 ★★★

Tin 30 x 20 x 4cm

This recipe makes a dainty little biscuit. It is quite crumbly but very delicious. If you want a thicker biscuit use a smaller tin. The four (!) layers make it a bit fiddly but they are worth it for special occasions.

The Base
- 150g flour
- 75g butter
- 15g sugar

The Filling
- 2 eggs separated
- 100g caster sugar
- 100g ground almonds
- ½ tsp almond essence

- 3 Tbs raspberry jam

- 60g flaked almonds

Pre-heat the oven to 160°C.

Line the tin with baking parchment leaving enough sticking up to help lift the slices out at the end.

Mix the ingredients for the base together in the food processor, press into the prepared tin using your hand and an extra sheet of parchment and bake for 20 minutes at 160°C.

Whisk the egg whites and when they hold peaks, whisk in a couple of tablespoons of the sugar.

Mix the rest of the sugar in a bowl with the ground almonds, lightly beaten egg yolks and essence.
This is quite thick.

Stir in about a quarter of the whites to soften the almond mixture and then fold in the rest more gently.

Spread the cooked base with jam and pour the topping onto it.

Scatter the flaked almonds on top.

Bake at 160°C for 30 to 40 minutes until golden brown.

Cool in the tin and cut into slices when cold.

Crispy Almond Biscuits

 ★

2-3 baking trays

This recipe makes about sixty delicious almond biscuits. They are very good if you have to bring biscuits to a party or other event. They keep well in a tin.

- 125g butter
- 250g caster sugar
- 1 egg
- 200g flour
- 50g semolina or ground rice
- 60g ground almonds
- 1 tsp baking powder
- 1 Tbs milk
- A handful of flaked almonds or some chopped glacé cherries

Pre-heat the oven to 165°C.

Line the trays with baking parchment.

Chop the butter into the food processor, add the sugar and mix until pale and smooth.

Then add the egg and beat until well mixed in.

Sieve the rest of the dry ingredients into a bowl and add to the butter mixture.

Add the milk and mix well. If the dough is too sticky to work add a little extra flour. Be careful not to add too much or the biscuits will not spread out nicely.

Roll into small walnut-sized balls and put onto trays, well spaced to allow for spreading.

Press a flaked almond or piece of cherry onto each biscuit.

Cook at 160°C for 15 to 20 minutes. They should be beginning to go golden.

Lift off the trays after a few minutes and cool on a wire rack. They will get crisp as they cool.

Spanish Almond Cake

**21cm diameter
loose-bottomed tin**

- 150g caster sugar
- 3 eggs separated
- 150g ground almonds

This is a light nutty cake with a faintly crisp top. It is very quick to make if you need something in a hurry. It is also very quick to eat…not something you would keep in a tin. Just eat it all in one go!

Pre-heat the oven to 170°C.

Grease the tin and line the base with baking parchment.

Whip the whites and when peaks form add 25g of the sugar gradually.

Beat until it is shiny.

Gently slide the whites into another bowl.

Beat the remaining 125g of the sugar with the egg yolks until quite pale.

Mix in the ground almonds slowly. This is now very thick.

Mix about a quarter of the whipped egg whites into the dough to loosen it. Then gently fold in the rest, taking care not to knock too much air out. It doesn't matter if there are some lumps.

Spread it into the tin and cook for 35 to 40 minutes at 170°C.

Leave for a few minutes before taking out of the tin. Then cool on a wire rack.

Honey and Almond Tart

25cm diameter loose-bottomed tin

This nutty tart has a gentle honey fragrance.
You can serve it as a dessert with whipped cream or make it on a tray and cut it into squares to use like a biscuit.

Base
- 170g flour
- 110g butter
- 30g caster sugar
- 1 egg yolk
- ½ tsp vanilla essence

Filling
- 1 Tbs honey
- 85g butter
- 45g soft light brown sugar
- 170g flaked almonds
- 1 Tbs cream

Pre-heat the oven to 160°C.

Grease the tin and line the base with baking parchment.

Process the flour and butter until like breadcrumbs.

Add in the sugar, mix a little and then add the egg yolk and vanilla. Mix until combined.

Press into the tin using your hand and an extra sheet of baking parchment, prick the surface and bake for 20 to 30 minutes or until becoming slightly golden.

While the base is cooking, make the filling.

Melt the honey, butter and sugar until bubbling gently.

Add the almonds and stir over a medium heat until the nuts are golden brown.

Stir in the cream and then pour the mixture on top of the cooked base.

Bake at 160°C until the nuts are dark golden. This will take 10 to 15 minutes.

Remove from the tin when cold.

Banana and Walnut Squares

Tin 30 x 20 x 4cm

I really love banana bread but find that because the mixture is very moist it is difficult to cook to the centre of a loaf. So I make it in the flat tin to get over that problem. It is quick and simple but goes stale quickly so I usually cut it into squares and freeze it as soon as it is cool. It is delicious heated up in the microwave.

- 100g butter
- 250g sugar
- 350g ripe bananas, peeled
- 2 eggs
- 250g self raising flour
- ½ tsp bread soda
- ¼ tsp salt
- 1 tsp baking powder
- 50g chopped walnuts

Pre-heat the oven to 160°C.

Line the tin with baking parchment leaving enough sticking up to help lift out the cake at the end.

Chop the butter into the food processor and cream with the sugar until soft.

Drop in the bananas one at a time and mix well.

Mix in the eggs one at a time.

Sieve all the dry ingredients except the walnuts into a big bowl.
Mix and then stir in the walnuts.

Stir the wet ingredients into the dry.
Pour into the tin and cook at 160°C for 45 minutes.
Cool in the tin and cut when cold.

Biscotti

2 baking trays

These traditional Italian biscuits are cooked twice; first in a log shape which is then cut into slices for the second baking. It feels strange using whole almonds but they look and taste lovely in the finished biscuit. The biscotti can be served dipped in coffee or dessert wine at the end of a meal.

The size of the eggs determines how sticky the dough will be and that determines how much the logs will spread out during the first stage. However, it is a very forgiving mixture and you can always add more flour if it is too wet to handle or a little milk if it is too dry. The biscuits keep well in a tin.

- 120g whole blanched almonds
- 3 small eggs or 2 large and ½ Tbs milk (see above)
- 1 tsp vanilla extract
- 300g plain flour
- 225g caster sugar
- ½ tsp baking powder
- Pinch salt

Pre heat oven to 160ºC.

Line the trays with baking parchment.

Grill the almonds until just brown. Cool completely.

Beat the eggs and vanilla in the mixer for a few minutes.

Add the flour, the sugar, the baking powder and the salt and beat fairly slowly.

When the dough forms a ball on the beaters add the almonds and mix in gently.

Scrape out the sticky batter onto a well floured table and divide it in two for ease of handling.

With floured hands, form each piece into a log about 25cm long (if you want smaller biscuits make the roll longer and thinner).

Place them on two parchment-covered baking trays. They will spread out.

Gently brush off any excess flour.

Bake for about 40 minutes at 160ºC until golden brown.

Put the logs onto a board and cut on the diagonal into 1cm slices.

Return them to the trays, and bake again at 160ºC for 10 minutes or so until hard and golden.

Cool on a wire rack.

You can also make these biscuits with hazel nuts or bits of dark chocolate.

Easy Peasy Brownies

Tin 30 x 20 x 4cm

These simple chocolate brownies are made with spelt flour which gives them a very smooth texture. If you want brownies, don't be tempted to replace the spelt with regular wheat flour or you will end up with chocolate cake. Also be careful not to overcook them, they should be quite sticky.

- 250g butter, softened
- 400g caster sugar
- 2 eggs
- 4 Tbs milk
- 1 tsp vanilla extract
- 150 white spelt flour
- 50g cocoa powder
- ¼ tsp salt
- 100g chopped pecans

Preheat the oven to 165°C.

Line the tin with baking parchment leaving enough sticking up to help lift the brownies out at the end.

Cream the butter and sugar with a beater until light and fluffy.

Add the eggs, milk and vanilla and beat well.

Sieve the spelt flour, cocoa and salt into a bowl and add to the creamed mixture.

Mix in slowly but thoroughly.

Mix in the nuts.

Spread the mixture into the tin. It is very thick but keep pushing at it with a spatula until it is as flat as you can get it on top.

Cook at 165°C for about 45 to 55 minutes or until the top is lightly crisp and a skewer comes out quite sticky.

Do not overcook, you really want that moist texture.

Cool in the tin, lift out and cut into squares on a board when cold.

Cashew Caramel Squares

 ★★★

Tin 30 x 20 x 4cm

I can't decide whether I like this better with peanuts, hazel or cashew nuts. Whichever nuts you choose, they must be skinned, roasted and unsalted! To skin raw peanuts or hazelnuts put them in a roasting pan under the grill until they are nicely browned. Then rub off the skins in a tea towel. If they are already skinned but raw, brown them under the grill. The biscuit base is quite soft and cake-like.

Base
- 125g butter
- 100g caster sugar
- 1 egg
- 225g plain flour
- 40g self raising flour
- 2 Tbs cornflour
- ½ tsp salt

Top
- 150g soft light brown sugar
- 65g golden syrup
- 180g butter
- 250g roasted, unsalted, cashews, hazel nuts or peanuts

Preheat the oven to 160°C.

Line the tin with baking parchment, leaving enough sticking up to help lift the squares out at the end.

In the processor cream the butter and sugar until fluffy.

Add the egg and mix well.

Sieve the dry ingredients into a bowl and then add to the butter mix. Process until combined.

Put the mixture into the lined tin and press down using your hand and an extra sheet of baking parchment.

Bake at 160°C for 30 minutes or until golden.

While the base is cooking make the topping.

Melt the sugar, syrup and butter and simmer for five minutes.

Stir in the nuts and bring back to the boil for a minute or two.

Pour the topping over the base when it is done and cook for a further 10 minutes until it is bubbling and browned.

Cool in the tin, lift out and cut on a board when cold.

Cheddar Cheese Biscuits

 ★★

2-3 baking trays

Use small fancy cutters and you have a great dinner party gift. I make a mixture of sun, moon and stars. They are delicious with a drink…buttery and cheesy. They keep quite well in a tin but you could also keep them in a box in the freezer so you can take out a handful whenever you want them.

- 120g plain flour
- ¼ tsp baking powder
- ½ tsp salt
- ¼ tsp cayenne pepper
- 125g butter
- 2 Tbs grated Parmesan
- 125g Dubliner or other strong cheddar cheese, grated
- 1 Tbs lemon juice

Preheat the oven to 160°C.

Line the trays with baking parchment.

Sieve the dry ingredients into a bowl and then put them into the food processor.

Chop in the butter and process until fine.

Add in the cheeses and mix to a soft dough. Put in half the lemon juice and if the mixture is on the dry side add the rest.

Roll out and cut, gathering up the edge bits and re-rolling them.

Then bake on parchment covered trays at 160°C for 10 to 15 minutes until golden brown.

Cool on wire racks.

Chocolate Amaretti Cake

21cm diameter loose-bottomed tin

You will have this Italian style cake in the oven within twenty minutes of starting the preparation (if you work quickly!). It has a grainy texture which you can make as coarse or as smooth as you like. It is a little bit plain to look at so I make a leaf stencil with icing sugar to cheer it up. Once you bite into it you will forget about the stencil and be transported straight to heaven.

- *150g dark chocolate*
- *50g amaretti biscuits*
- *100g flaked almonds*
- *175g caster sugar*
- *zest of one orange*
- *100g butter*
- *4 eggs beaten*
- *icing sugar for dusting*
- *A pretty leaf*

Preheat the oven to 170°C.

Line the base of the tin with baking parchment and butter the sides well.

Melt the chocolate in a bowl over, but not touching, simmering water.

Put the biscuits, almonds, sugar and zest into the food processor and whizz until almost ground but still gritty. Check it by tasting (yum). This will be the texture of the finished cake.

Chop in the butter and add the eggs.
Whizz until blended.

Add the chocolate and whizz until blended again.

Pour the mixture into the tin and cook at 170°C for 35 minutes until the cake is puffed up and slightly cracked.

Remove from the oven and let it rest for 15 minutes in the tin before transferring it to the serving plate.

It will sink and crack more as it cools.

Sprinkle with icing sugar just before serving. I like it best a tiny bit warm with a blob of whipped cream but it is fine served completely cold... very good with strawberries.

Christmas Biscuits

2-3 baking trays

Many of these gingerbread-house style biscuit doughs are easy to work but haven't got a great flavour or texture when cooked. So I was delighted to find this recipe as it combines ease of working with a great flavour. Now you can have your house and eat it! You can also hang them on the Christmas tree though this is not recommended for damp houses where they will plop onto the floor and be eaten by the dog.

- 60g butter
- 75g caster sugar
- 2½ Tbs cream
- 1½ Tbs black treacle
- 2 tsp ground cinnamon
- 2 tsp ground ginger
- ½ tsp ground cloves
- seeds of 4 cardamom pods ground
- zest of one small orange
- 185g plain flour
- ¼ tsp bread soda

Preheat the oven to 160°C.

Line the trays with baking parchment.

Warm butter, sugar, cream, treacle, cinnamon, ginger, cloves, cardamom and orange zest over a low heat until the butter is melted and the sugar dissolved. Let it come to the bubble and then take it off the heat.

Sieve the flour and soda together into a bowl and add to the pan, stirring to form a dough. Knead on a lightly floured surface. It is very soft but firms as it cools.

Wrap in cling film and chill for at least 1 hour.

Bring back to room temperature and roll out to the thickness of a euro coin.

Cut into Christmas shapes making a small hole in the top if you are going to hang them up.

Bake on parchment-lined trays at 160°C for 10 to 12 minutes.

Cool on a wire rack

When cool decorate with water icing:
Sieve ½ cup of icing sugar into a bowl. Add a little water and stir. Keep adding water slowly until you get the consistency you want.

If you want to make a gingerbread house you will need to double the recipe.

Citrus Cake

21cm diameter loose-bottomed tin

I have tried many of these orange cakes, some involving boiling the oranges for ages and removing the pips from the hot flesh. Ouch! This is the simplest recipe I have found. I have reduced the oil a little from its original as I feel the syrup keeps it all moist enough. And I would prefer juicy fingers to oily fingers. You could also serve it with cream as a dessert.

If you add the juice to the cake mix by mistake instead of keeping it for the syrup, just reduce the cooking temperature, increase the time and watch that it doesn't burn at the edge. It works, I know.

- 50g stale bread
- 200g caster sugar
- 100g ground almonds
- 1 ½ tsp baking powder
- zest of a large orange and lemon
- 100ml sunflower oil
- 4 eggs

Syrup
- juice of the orange and lemon
- 75g caster sugar
- 2 cloves
- 1 short cinnamon stick
- a few cardamom pods or crushed seeds (optional)

No need to pre-heat oven.

Grease the tin and line the base with parchment.

Make the bread into crumbs in the food processor and then mix in the sugar, almonds, baking powder and zest.

Whisk the eggs lightly with the oil and add to the dry ingredients in the processor.

Whizz until mixed.

Pour into the tin and put in a cold oven set to 175°C.

Cook for 50 to 60 mins until a skewer comes out clean.

While the cake is cooking simmer the syrup ingredients together for a few minutes.

When the cake is cooked pierce it all over and strain the syrup over the top arranging the cinnamon and cloves as decoration.

Remove from the tin when cold.

Coconut Macaroons

2-3 baking trays

I like the fact that these macaroons use the whole egg so you don't have a white or yolk going hard in a cup in the fridge. They are light and gluten free and keep well in a tin. Makes about 50.

- *2 eggs separated*
- *pinch salt*
- *150g sugar*
- *275g desiccated coconut*

Preheat the oven to 160°C.

Line the trays with baking parchment.

Beat the egg whites and salt until they make soft peaks.

Beat in yolks one at a time.

Add sugar slowly and beat until dissolved, then speed up for a few minutes until it is light and fluffy.

Stir in the coconut.

Spoon large teaspoonfuls onto baking trays leaving room for them to spread out a bit.

Bake 160°C for 15 to 20 minutes.

Cool on wire rack.

Coconut Slices

Tin 30 x 20 x 4cm

This is a rather crumbly delicious fruit slice. The brown flour gives it a slightly crunchy texture and makes it full of goodness.

It keeps better frozen than in a tin.

- 125g butter
- 125g soft brown sugar
- 3 eggs
- 100ml milk
- 125g brown flour
- 125g dried coconut
- 1 tsp baking powder
- 1 tsp mixed spice
- 185g dried fruit

Preheat the oven to 160°C.

Line the tin with baking parchment leaving enough sticking up to help lift out the slices at the end.

Cream the butter and sugar in the processor.

Beat in the eggs and milk.

Put the dry ingredients in a bowl, mix well and then stir in the egg mixture.

Pour it into the tin and flatten it out with a spatula.

Bake at 160°C for about 35 to 40 minutes.

Leave to cool in the tin and then cut into squares.

Date Slices

 ★★★

Tin 30 x 20 x 4cm

This makes a slice with a big thick date layer in between two thin layers of biscuit. You could halve the amount of filling and it would still be fine but not as deliciously squidgy.

Keeps best in the freezer.

Date filling
- 750g stoned dates
- 50g white sugar
- 325ml water

Biscuit top and bottom
- 200g butter
- 185g light brown sugar
- 4 Tbs milk
- 1 egg
- 270g plain flour
- 1 tsp salt
- ½ tsp bread soda
- 150g oatmeal

Preheat the oven to 160°C.

Line the tin with baking parchment leaving enough sticking up to help lift out the slices at the end.

The dates are really easy to process once they are cooked so get them started before you make the biscuit part.

Put the ingredients for the filling into a saucepan, bring to the boil and simmer until soft. This only takes a few minutes. Allow to cool a little.

Cream the butter and sugar in the food processor and then add the egg and milk.

Sieve the flour, salt and bread soda into a bowl and add to the butter mix. Process until smooth.

Then add the oatmeal and whizz briefly. Put into a bowl.

Put the soft date mixture into the processor (no need to wash out) and whizz until smooth.

Put half the biscuit mixture into the tin and press down well using your hand and an extra sheet of baking parchment.

Spread the date mixture over the base and carefully top off with the rest of the biscuit mix. This is quite difficult and it helps to put it on in little blobs and then press down with a sheet of parchment.

Cook at 160°C for 50 to 60 minutes until golden.

When it is completely cold, lift the cake out onto a board and cut into thick slices using a very sharp knife.

Lavistown Flapjacks

Tray 32 x 23 cm

- 125g butter
- 100g margarine
- 130g caster sugar
- 80g golden syrup
- 75g sesame seeds
- 350g oatmeal

These crispy biscuits are a cross between a sesame snap and a true flapjack. They have always been very popular; tasty and sustaining. I find using half margarine gives them a better texture than all butter.

They are very quick and simple to make and will keep for ages in a tin.

Preheat the oven to 160°C and line the baking trays with baking parchment leaving enough sticking up to help lift out the flapjacks at the end.

Melt the fat, sugar, syrup and seeds gently in a big pot over a medium heat and stir until the fat and sugar are melted and the whole thing is bubbling gently all over.

Take off the heat and stir in the oatmeal.

Spread onto the tray and press down firmly using another sheet of parchment under your hand to get a good compact structure.

Cook at 160°C for about 35 minutes, until dark golden.

After about 10 minutes, cut into squares before cold and set.

Allow them to cool completely before taking off the tray.

Ginger Jumblies

2 baking trays

These biscuits are great to make with kids as the dough has a lovely texture and can be rolled into balls or snakes to make round or long biscuits. They can be cooked to be soft and spongy or dry and crisp. If left in the tin, the dry and crisp ones become soft and spongy very quickly.

The rather strange icing gives them a sheen reminiscent of biscuits in the sixties.

- 60g butter
- 250g syrup
- 230g plain flour
- 1 tsp bread soda
- 1 tsp ground ginger
- 1 tsp mixed spice
- ½ tsp ground cloves
- 1 Tbs milk

Icing
- 1 egg white
- 55g icing sugar, sifted
- 2 tsp plain flour, sifted
- 2 tsp approx lemon juice

Preheat the oven to 160°C.

Line the trays with baking parchment.

Melt the butter and syrup in a saucepan and bring to the boil.

Turn off the heat and let it stand for 10 minutes.

Sieve the dry ingredients and add to the syrup mix.

Add the milk and stir until smooth.

Let it stand for 2 hours, covered.

Knead into little balls or snakes and flatten them out a bit, flouring your hands if necessary.

Put on baking trays 3 to 4 cm apart.

Cook at 160°C for 20 minutes or longer if you want them crisp.

Remove from tray while still warm and cool on a wire rack.

They are lovely on their own but if you want to ice them, prepare the icing so that it is ready to put on the biscuits while they are warm.

Mix the icing sugar into the egg white in three lots and then mix in the flour.

Stir in enough lemon juice to make a spreading consistency.

Spread the icing over the biscuits and put them back into the oven for two minutes or until the icing feels firm.

Leave to cool on the tray and trim any icing that has run off when they are cool.

Muriel's Gingerbread

Tin 30 x 20 x 4cm

This is a variation of my mother's gingerbread recipe. She was quite inventive in the kitchen but her recipe for gingerbread never changed. I have just put in some brown flour and added the syrup and chopped ginger.

It doesn't keep all that well in a tin but is delicious heated from frozen, in a microwave.

- 85g black treacle
- 85g golden syrup
- 100g butter
- 250ml water

- 175g plain white flour
- 175g brown flour
- 50g sugar
- 1 heaped tsp dried ginger sieved
- 1 heaped tsp bread soda sieved
- 60g crystalline ginger chopped coarsely

Preheat the oven to 160°C.

Line the tin with baking parchment leaving enough sticking up to help lift the gingerbread out at the end.

Heat the treacle, syrup, butter and water in a saucepan until melted together.

Mix the remaining ingredients in a big bowl and then stir in the mix from the saucepan.

Pour into the prepared tin and bake at 160°C for 35 to 45 minutes or until a skewer comes out clean.

Let it cool in the tin.

Granola Bars

 ★★★

Tin 32 x 20cm

These fantastic bars are full of chewy goodness to sustain you for hours. They are more for outdoors than for afternoon tea. On a recent canoeing trip we discovered that if they get wet they return rather unpleasantly to their original ingredients!

They are made by toasting the dry ingredients and then sticking them together with a 'glue' mixture. They are not cooked again. They take a bit of time to make due to the chopping and toasting but they are well worth it.

They keep for ages in a tin.

- 200g oatmeal
- 100g mixed seeds: sesame, pumpkin, sunflower
- 125g coarsely chopped toasted hazelnuts*
- 85g wheatgerm or oat bran

Glue
- 120g soft brown sugar
- 150g honey
- 75g butter
- 1 tsp vanilla
- ½ tsp salt

- 125g chopped apricots
- 100g chopped dates

* These may need to be skinned first by toasting them and rubbing the skins off in a rough tea towel.

Line the tin with baking parchment leaving enough sticking up to help lift the bars out at the end.

Spread the oatmeal, seeds and nuts in a roasting pan and put under the grill until beginning to colour... about ten minutes.

Watch carefully and don't let them burn. Stir a couple of times during the toasting.

Add in the wheatgerm or oat bran for about five minutes more.

Now make the glue.

Melt the ingredients for the glue in a saucepan and simmer for about five minutes.

Mix the toasted dry ingredients with the apricots and dates and then stir in the 'glue' from the saucepan. It feels as if it is not going to all mix in but keep stirring and eventually it will become incorporated.

Spread it into the prepared tin and press down hard and evenly all over the surface of the granola using another sheet of parchment paper under your hand.

Leave to cool.

When completely cold put it onto a board and cut into bars.

Hazelnut Cookies

 ★★

2-3 baking trays

The icing sugar in these biscuits gives them a very smooth texture contrasting with the nuts. They are lovely dusted with more icing sugar and taste unexpectedly delicious. They keep well in a tin.

- *150g hazelnuts, skinned, roasted and cooled**
- *250g butter*
- *80g icing sugar*
- *90g honey*
- *300g plain flour*

- *Icing sugar for dusting*

* If the nuts are not already prepared, grill them until quite brown but be careful not to burn them. Rub off the skins in a tea towel and grind when cool.

Preheat the oven to 160°C.

Line the trays with baking parchment.

Grind hazelnuts coarsely in a food processor and put into a bowl.

Chop the butter into the processor and mix in the sugar until light and fluffy.

Mix in the honey and then the flour and nuts.

With floured hands roll teaspoonfuls into balls. They are quite sticky and you may need to flour your fingers to manage them.

Place on lined trays 1.5 cms apart.

Bake at 160°C for 15-20 minutes. They do not spread out very much but stay as humpy little biscuits.

Cool on a wire rack and serve dusted with more icing sugar.

Honey Cake

n 30 x 20 x 4cm
21cm diameter
ose-bottomed tin

The Kilkenny Bee Keepers keep their hives here at Lavistown and supply us with delicious honey which couldn't be purer or more local. This easy cake is moist and sticky with a lovely subtle honey flavour. If you cook it for a shorter time you will get an almost fudge-like layer at the bottom.

It keeps quite well in the tin

350g honey
300g butter
170g light brown soft sugar
1 Tbs water
400g self raising flour sieved
4 eggs beaten

ing
100g icing sugar
2 Tbs honey
2 Tbs lemon juice

Preheat the oven to 160°C.

Line the tin with baking parchment leaving the enough sticking up to help lift out the cake at the end.

Melt honey, butter, sugar and water in a large saucepan.

Remove from heat and beat in flour and eggs.

Pour into prepared tin and bake for 45 minutes at 160°C. If you want the fudge layer take it out after about 35 minutes. You can test with a skewer and choose which you prefer.

Cool in the tin and then cut into slices.

This is lovely as it is but if you want to go the extra mile, ice while it is still warm.

Sieve the icing sugar and then mix with the other ingredients. Spread over the cake while it is still warm.

Kate's Lemon Bars

Tin 30 x 20 x 4 cm

People's eyes glaze over when they take the first bite of these delicious slices. They are tangy and buttery with a curd topping. The top is the tricky part but it is well worth the effort. They freeze well.

Base
- 250g plain flour
- 175g butter
- 85g caster sugar

Top
- juice and rind of two lemons
- 3 eggs
- 300g caster sugar
- 50g plain flour
- ¾ tsp sieved baking powder
- ¼ tsp salt

Preheat the oven to 160°C.

Line the tin with baking parchment leaving enough sticking up to help lift out the bars out at the end.

Process the ingredients for the base and put into the tin, pressing down firmly using an extra sheet of baking parchment paper under your hand.

Cook at 160°C for 20 to 30 minutes until beginning to go golden.

Remove from the oven and turn down heat to 150°C.

While the base is cooking prepare the top

Grate and juice the lemons into a large bowl.

Add the eggs and mix with a whisk just enough to make it smooth and without streaks of egg white. Do not whip.

Weigh out the dry ingredients in a separate bowl.

As soon as the base is cooked and out of the oven, stir the dry ingredients into the eggs and lemon. Use the whisk again but mix gently until everything is incorporated and smooth. You do not want to beat air into it.

Pour it onto the base and put it into the cooled oven (150°C) for 20 - 25 minutes… keep touching it with your fingers to see if it is set.

When you take it from the oven the top should be just set and beginning to go golden. This gives a lemon curdy top; if you want it to be firmer cook at a higher temperature.

Cool in the tin and then cut into bars and serve dusted with icing sugar.

Basic Muffins

  ★

12 hole silicone muffin tray or metal muffin tray and liners

Muffins are very quick to make. Once you get used to making the basic type you can experiment with flavours both sweet and savoury. You can rub in the butter by hand or in a food processor but when you are stirring in the sugar, milk and egg do it lightly with a wooden spoon. The mixture should be quite lumpy.

Basic type
- *375g self raising flour*
- *90g butter*
- *220g castor sugar*
- *310ml buttermilk*
- *1 egg lightly beaten*

Preheat the oven to 160°C.

If using a metal muffin tray, line with paper or silicone cases.

Sieve the flour and rub in butter by hand or in the processor.

Stir in the sugar, buttermilk and egg.

Spoon into the muffin cases and cook at 160°C for about 40 minutes.

Variations

Try adding raisins, spices, chopped nuts etc for variation.

For lemon muffins add the rind and juice of two lemons and 50g of poppy seeds and cook for a little longer.

Chocolate Muffins

For chocolate muffins I have changed the basic recipe a bit. The use of spelt flour and the absence of the egg makes the texture really soft.

12 hole silicone muffin tray or metal muffin tray and liners

- *200g self raising flour*
- *100g white spelt flour*
- *125g butter*
- *50g cocoa*
- *275g caster sugar*
- *330ml buttermilk*
- *75g dark chocolate, chopped into small pieces*

Preheat the oven to 160°C.

If using a metal muffin tray, line with paper or silicone cases.

Sieve the flours and rub in the butter by hand or in the processor.

Sieve the cocoa and mix in well.

Stir in the sugar, buttermilk and lastly the chocolate.

Fill the muffin tray and cook at 160°C for about 40 minutes.

I particularly like these muffins warmed in the microwave so that the chocolate melts... but not everyone agrees with that.

Oatmeal Muffins

We got the original recipe for these muffins from an oatmeal bag in Canada about forty years ago. Unfortunately we lost it so this is an attempt at a reincarnation. I think it is pretty close.

12 hole silicone muffin tray or metal muffin tray and liners

- *200g self raising flour*
- *90g butter*
- *175g oatmeal*
- *220g caster sugar*
- *100g raisins*
- *460ml buttermilk*
- *1 egg*
- *½ tsp vanilla essence*

Preheat the oven to 160°C.

If using a metal muffin tray, line with paper or silicone cases.

Sieve the flour and rub in the butter by hand or in the processor. Then stir in the sugar, oatmeal and raisins in a bowl.

Beat the egg lightly with the buttermilk and vanilla and add to the dry ingredients. Mix gently together.

Spoon the mixture into the lined bun cases and put them in the oven at 160°C.

You will need to cook them for almost an hour.

Simple Shortbread Biscuits

 ★

2-3 baking trays

As the name implies these are very simple shortbread biscuits...sweet and buttery but with a crunchy bite from the semolina. They can be a bit tricky to roll out but warm hands help the mixture to stick together.

- *200g butter*
- *100g sugar*
- *225g plain flour*
- *100g semolina or ground rice*

- *flaked almonds (optional)*

Preheat the oven to 160°C.

Line the trays with baking parchment.

Cream the butter and sugar well in the food processor.

Add in the flour and semolina and mix again.

You may need to add a little more flour. The dough should hold together well and not be sticky or crumbly.

Put it onto a floured surface and divide into three pieces for ease of handling.

Roll it out quite thinly, about the thickness of a coin, and cut into whatever shapes you like. Gather up the edge bits and roll again.

Use whatever cutters you like; they look good as stars or classic little round biscuits, perhaps with an almond pressed into the top before baking.

Bake at 160°C until they have the slightest brown tinge.

Cool on a wire rack.

They are nice dusted with icing sugar.

Tea Brack

3 loaf tins
23 x 11 x 6 cms

I feel if you are going to the trouble of the overnight soaking and having the oven on for ages you might as well make a big batch of this traditional moist tea brack. This recipe makes three loaves. They keep well wrapped in foil or for longer in the freezer.

I have left the measurements for this recipe in cups as this is how it came to me and it is very handy. It is all a matter of proportions so it doesn't matter about the size of the cup! I have included the metric measurements.

- 3 cups sultanas (400g)
- 2 cups raisins (280g)
- 1 cup peel and chopped cherries mixed (175g)
- 1 cup chopped walnuts (120g)
- 2 cups soft brown sugar (350g)
- 3 cups black tea (700ml)

- 4 cups plain flour (420g)
- 3 tsp baking powder
- 3 tsp mixed spice
- 3 beaten eggs

Sticky glaze
- 2 Tbs sugar
- 2 Tbs water

Preheat the oven to 160°C.

Grease the sides of the tins and line the bases with baking parchment allowing some to stick out at each end for lifting out the loaves after baking.

Soak the fruit, nuts and sugar in the tea overnight in a big bowl.

Next day sieve the flour, baking powder and spices. Mix and add them in two or three batches to the fruit mix, alternating with the beaten eggs.

Pour into the prepared tins and spread out evenly.

Bake at 160°C for 1¾ hours or until a skewer comes out clean.

Then lift out using the ends of the lining paper and cool on a wire rack.

To make the glaze, bring the sugar and water slowly to the boil in a small saucepan until the sugar has dissolved.

Simmer gently for 2-3 minutes and paint onto the loaves when they are cool.

White Chocolate and Apricot Cookies

 ★★

2-3 baking trays

These are made in the same way as the ready-made cookie dough you can buy. Have a couple of these rolls in the fridge and you can cook delicious biscuits in a jiffy.

Rather like muffins, when you get the hang of making the basic ones you can have fun trying lots of variations.

- *110g butter softened*
- *160g caster sugar*
- *1 tsp vanilla essence*
- *1 egg beaten*
- *175g plain flour*
- *1 tsp baking powder*
- *100g white chocolate pellets or chopped up bar*
- *50g dried apricots finely chopped*

Preheat the oven to 170°C.

Line the trays with baking parchment.

In the processor, mix together butter, sugar and vanilla until light and fluffy.

Add the egg to the butter mix.

Sieve the flour and baking powder into a bowl and add it to the butter mix.

Fold in the chocolate and apricots by hand.

Divide the dough into two and roll in cling film into two sausages about 4 cms in diameter. It is very soft at this stage but don't worry, it will firm up as it cools.

Chill in the fridge.

Cut into 1cm slices and place on the trays 5 to 6 cm apart.
The thicker the slices the bigger the biscuit.

Cook for about 15 minutes until turning golden.

Cool on a wire rack.

You could also try milk chocolate and raisins for kids or dark chocolate and dried cranberries with rum replacing the vanilla for grown ups at Christmas.

BREADS

Despite my passion for making yeast bread this is not a book which will teach you all the steps of this fascinating process. Making bread with yeast is very easy but it helps enormously to see someone do it and then make it alongside them for the first time.

The best way to learn is to go on a course…a day is good, but even a morning will teach you enough to get you started. For a step by step guide the best book I have found is The River Cottage Handbook, No.3 Bread. Also of course there is YouTube which will make bread before your very eyes in your own kitchen.

Briefly, you mix flour, water, yeast and a little salt in a bowl and knead it with your hands until it all comes together in a smooth stretchy ball. Then you leave it to rise for an hour or so in a warm place until it is double in volume. This is called proving.

Knowing when the dough is 'double in volume' is the most difficult part. It should be really soft and puffy when you poke it with your finger. If it feels a bit firm leave it longer and if it has over-risen and the air is escaping in all directions fear not. Shove it all back into the bowl and proceed with the knocking back process.

Knocking back happens after the first rising. What you do is squeeze out all the precious air... it seems a bit pointless but it helps in the development of the gluten to make a strong dough. Then shape your loaves, leave them to rise again and then bake them.

The dough literally has a life of its own and produces, at the end of the day, a delicious, nutritious loaf to put on the table. Bread is at its best when it is very fresh so if I make extra I freeze it as soon as it is cold and then heat it up in the microwave. This doesn't work very well with foccacia due to its oiliness so just let it thaw naturally.

I have included four main recipes; one is dead simple, one is a rich version of this dough and the other two I have learnt or developed over the years and are part of my life. There are also recipes and ideas for nice things to do with these doughs. When you are happy with these basic recipes you can try more detailed ones from other sources.

Notes
- *The words 'strong' or 'bread' must appear on the flour bag.*
  This means the flour has more gluten than all-purpose flour so is good for trapping air.
- *The water should feel comfortably warm to your fingers.*
- *The yeast in these recipes is fast acting dried yeast. It is a powder made up of yeast cells and nutrients. The yeast cells are alive and when they get warm and wet they wake up they start to breathe. This releases carbon dioxide which gets trapped in the dough making it light and airy.*
- *The ideal temperature for rising is that in which is comfortable for you to wear a T shirt. It doesn't matter if it is cooler, it will just rise more slowly.*

Versatile Plain Dough

 ★★★

This is a very straightforward dough which has many uses. It is a great one to start with as it is simple to knead and you can use it in many different ways.

- *500g strong white flour*
- *1 sachet fast action yeast*
- *2 tsp salt*
- *2 Tbs olive oil*
- *325ml warm water*

Mix the dry ingredients together and make a well in the centre.

Add the water and the oil.

Stir in and when it becomes too stiff, start to knead by hand.

Knead for ten minutes until it is smooth and elastic, flouring your hands lightly if they get sticky.

Cover with oiled cling film* and a tea towel and leave to rise in a warm place until doubled in volume and soft to the touch. This process is called proving.

When it is well risen knock it back (see page 63) until it feels firm again.

This dough is now ready to make loaves, rolls, flatbread, pizza, foccacia etc.

*A good way is to put the cling film on the dough ball, spread on the oil with your fingers and then turn the cling film over so the oily side is down. Leave it loose enough to allow the dough to rise.

Versatile Plain Dough Uses

 ★★★

Try any of these ideas which will bring a gorgeous aroma to your kitchen and smiles of appreciation all round.

Rolls
After the first rising knock back the dough and then weigh out 80g balls and shape until smooth tucking any joins underneath. Paint with water and then sprinkle seeds on top or glaze with egg wash or dredge flour on top through a sieve. Place close together on a lined baking sheet. Let rise until they are big and soft and touching each other and then bake at 200°C for about 35 minutes or until dark golden brown.

Pizza
Roll it out as thinly as you can, patching it if you make a tear. Stretch further on a pizza tray or baking sheet lightly dusted with flour or semolina. You should get two 30cm pizzas from one batch of dough. Put on your chosen sauce and toppings and before it rises any more put straight into the hottest oven you can make for 10 to 15 minutes.

Flatbreads
Roll out small pieces of risen dough quite thinly and dry-fry quickly in a hot dry pan. These are great for sharing round the table with a bottle of wine and hummus, guacamole, sundried tomato pesto, etc.

Tear 'n' Share
Knock back after the first rising and then tear off golf ball sized pieces of dough. Nestle them together in an oiled pie tin. Leave to rise, paint with olive oil (for a soft roll) or water (for a crisper crust) and bake at 200°C for 30 minutes. Great with soups and stews.

Foccacia
Knock back and push out into a 25cm round tin. After the second rise dimple the surface deeply with the fingers, paint very generously with olive oil, sprinkle with sea salt and leave to rise again before baking at 200°C for 35 minutes.

Lavistown Loaves

 ★★★

Loaf tins or
shape as you wish

This is our everyday bread at Lavistown….full of seeds and treacle. I make it as small round loaves (like enormous buns) fitting snugly into a roasting tin. Make them whatever size and shape suits you…either in loaf tins or on a baking sheet or roasting tin. I usually make double this recipe at a time. Then I freeze the loaves and heat them in the microwave for two minutes when I need them.

- *425g strong white flour*
- *250g brown flour or strong brown*
- *50g oat bran or wheatgerm or a mixture of both*
- *1 Tbs salt*
- *1 sachet fast action yeast*
- *25g each of linseed/sesame/ sunflower seeds*
- *550ml warm water*
- *40g black treacle*
- *2 Tbs sunflower oil*

Mix all the dry ingredients in a large bowl.

Dissolve the treacle in some boiling water and then make it up to 550ml with lukewarm water. This is a messy business but the amount of treacle is not critical so if you have extra sticking to the spoon don't worry.

Stir the water, treacle and oil into the flour mixture.

When stirring becomes too difficult knead with floured hands. This is supposed to be a soft dough so add as little extra flour as possible.

Leave to rise until doubled in size, then knock back.

Put into oiled loaf tins or shape as you wish, cover and leave to rise.

Bake at 210°C for 10 minutes and then at 190°C for a further 40 minutes or until it looks done and sounds hollow when tapped on the bottom.

Brush with milk and cool on a wire rack.

Mama's Bread

 ★★★

Tin 32 x 21cm

- *500g strong flour*
- *½ sachet fast action yeast*
- *1 tsp salt*
- *325ml warm water*

I learned how to make this ciabatta style bread from an Italian friend; it is the bread his mother makes. It makes an impressive loaf which is great with soup or dips and is also perfect for bruschetta. It just has one rise which results in lots of irregularly sized holes.

Mix the flour, salt and yeast.

Stir in the water gradually and then start to knead the dough.

As it becomes sticky, instead of adding flour, dip your hand in warm water and continue to knead.

Keep adding more water with your hand until the dough is very stretchy and loose and sticky, more like a batter than a dough. It will take about 100ml extra water.

Spread it into an oiled and lined roasting tin and flatten out the surface, again using wet hands.

Cover it with a tray, inverted roasting tin or oiled cling film. You do not want the rising dough to touch this cover as it is very sticky.

Put it somewhere warm and when it is well risen with bubbles beginning to show on top, dust it liberally with flour through a sieve.

Bake at 200°C for 25 - 30 minutes until browned and sounds hollow when tapped on the bottom.

Versatile Rich Dough

 ★★★

This is like the previous dough but it is enriched with egg, butter and milk. I like to use some plain flour along with the strong as it gives the finished product a softer more cake-like texture. It is slower to rise than the plain dough.

- *300g strong flour*
- *200g plain flour*
- *100g caster sugar*
- *1 sachet fast action dried yeast*
- *¼ tsp salt*
- *270ml milk*
- *80g butter cut up small*
- *1 egg*

Mix the dry ingredients together in a bowl.

Warm the milk and butter gently to blood heat.
A microwave is helpful here if you have one.
Make sure that it is finger warm and then beat in the egg.

Mix the milk mixture into the dry ingredients and stir until it comes together.

Knead by hand adding more flour if it is too sticky.
The dough should be quite soft so try not to add too much flour.

Leave to rise and then use it for sweet recipes such as cinnamon swirls, almond ring or hot cross buns.

Cinnamon Swirls

22cm square ceramic dish lined with parchment.

These buns tear apart and should be served while still warm from the oven. They are not very pretty but sticky and sweet and quite delicious. Try to remember to take off a third of the dough to spread over the bottom of the dish as this soaks up any of the sugary butter that seeps out. If you forget (we have all done that) just continue on and your buns will be a bit bigger. In that case perhaps turn down the heat to prevent the bottom burning and cook for a bit longer.

One batch of Rich Versatile Dough - see page 73

Filling
- 75g softned butter
- 100g sugar
- ¾ tsp cinnamon

Glaze
- 1 egg
- 3 Tbs milk

Line the dish with baking parchment, leaving enough sticking up to help with lifting the buns out at the end.

While the dough is rising, mix the filling ingredients together.

When the dough is well risen, take off a third of it and stretch it into the bottom of the dish.

Roll out the rest of the dough into a rectangle roughly 30 x 25 cm. Try to get the edges straight.

Spread the filling over the dough, right to the edges. Roll it up like a swiss roll starting with a long side.

Using a scissors, cut into 16 equal sized buns. An easy way to do this is to cut the roll in half again and again until you have 16 pieces.

Place four rows of four onto the dough base.

Leave (covered in butter paper) to rise again until they fit snugly together and are soft and puffy.

Cook at 190°C for 10 minutes then turn down the heat to 185°C for 25 - 30 minutes until they are golden. If they start to get quite dark on top but still look pale between the buns, turn down the heat and leave in the oven for a bit longer.

Mix the glaze ingredients, paint the buns generously and then put them back in the oven for 5 minutes.

Lift out of the dish all in one piece and cool on a wire rack.

Serve while still warm.

Hot Cross Buns

 ★★★

Baking tray

The spicy smell of these traditional buns wafting through your house will get Easter off to a good start. Of course you can make them without the crosses for sticky buns throughout the year.

One batch of Rich Versatile Dough - see page 73 - made with one heaped teaspoonful of mixed spice added to the dry ingredients.

Fruit
- *50g raisins*
- *50g mixed peel*

For the crosses
- *4 Tbs flour*
- *1 Tbs caster sugar*
- *2-3 Tbs water*

Sticky glaze
- *2 Tbs sugar*
- *2 Tbs water*

Preheat the oven to 200°C.
Line the tray with baking parchment.

Make the enriched dough remembering to add the spice.

When it is well risen knock back and gently knead in the fruit until it is well distributed.

This is a little tricky but persevere.

Divide the dough into 16 even pieces and form into neat balls picking off any escaping fruit to prevent it burning.

Place close together on the tray.

Leave in a warm place until risen again and touching.

While you are waiting for the buns to rise, make the paste for the crosses.

Mix the flour and sugar with enough water to make a thick piping consistency.

When the buns are risen pipe the paste onto them and put them into the oven.

Bake at 200°C for 10 minutes lowering the temperature then to 190°C for about 25 minutes more.

To make the glaze, bring the sugar and water slowly to the boil in a small saucepan until the sugar has dissolved.

Simmer gently for 2-3 minutes and paint onto the loaves when they are cool.

Glaze the buns when they have cooled a little.

Almond Ring

 ★★★

Baking tray

This cake is reminiscent of Bewley's in the old days. It combines my favourite ingredients… rich yeast dough, toasted almonds and a delicious marzipan filling. The only problem is, no matter how hard you try to keep the filling in the middle, it always sinks to the bottom.

One batch of risen Rich Versatile Dough
- see page 73

Almond paste
- 100g caster sugar
- 150g icing sugar sieved
- 225g ground almonds
- 1 beaten egg
- ½ tsp lemon juice

Egg wash
- 1 egg
- 3 Tbs milk

Sticky glaze
- 2 Tbs sugar
- 2 Tbs water

Preheat the oven to 190°C and line the tray with baking parchment.

To make the almond paste, mix the sugars and ground almonds together.

Stir in the beaten egg and lemon juice and squeeze into a smooth ball.

Wrap in cling film and put in the fridge until ready to use.

Roll out the risen dough into a rectangle roughly 30 x 25cm.

Make a 30cm sausage of the almond paste and lay it a few centimetres in from one long side.

Roll it up swiss roll style from this long edge.

Then gently pull the roll into a ring, tucking the edge underneath and squeezing the ends together as seamlessly as possible. Place on the tray.

Make the egg wash by beating the egg and milk together.

Let the dough rise again until it is soft then brush gently with the wash and bake at 190°C for 10 minutes.

Lower the temperature to 180°C for about another 25 minutes. Keep an eye on it and turn down the temperature more if it gets too brown.

Cool on a wire rack.

To make the glaze, bring the sugar and water slowly to the boil in a small saucepan until the sugar has dissolved.

Simmer gently for 2-3 minutes. Glaze the ring when it has cooled a little and sprinkle on some toasted flaked almonds. For a really nice finish you can glaze again on top of the nuts.

Stop Press!
Foolproof Ice Cream

Freezer-proof container

Just in case you need a simple ice cream for serving with disasters here is the quintessential recipe.

- 250ml whipping cream
- 450g jar of apricot jam
- juice of ½ a lemon
- 2 Tbs rum or amaretto liqueur
- 5 amaretti biscuits

Whip the cream to the soft peak stage and gently fold in the jam with a spoon.

When it is almost fully mixed in add the lemon juice and liqueur and crumble in the biscuits.

Fold it all together and pour into a freezer-proof container.

That's it!

Leave for at least six hours before serving. No need to stir or beat during freezing.

Very simple, very good.